English Springer Spaniel
A Working & Winning Show Dog Breed

Copyright © 2021

All rights reserved.

DEDICATION

The author and publisher have provided this e-book to you for your personal use only. You may not make this e-book publicly available in any way. Copyright infringement is against the law. If you believe the copy of this e-book you are reading infringes on the author's copyright, please notify the publisher at: https://us.macmillan.com/piracy

English Springer Spaniel

Contents

Breed Overview 1

History of the English Springer Spaniel 5

General Appearance 8

Temperament and Personality 13

Your English Springer Spaniel's Health .. 17

English Springer Spaniel Care 39

How much does an English Springer Spaniel cost?   44

How to Identify an English Springer Spaniel   51

English Springer Spaniel

Breed Overview

Country of Origin   England

Nicknames and Other Names   Springer Spaniel

Scientific Name   Canis lupus familiaris

Breed Type   Spaniel

English Springer Spaniel

Group	Sporting Dog, Gun Dog
Bred For	Flushing and retrieving gam
Size	Medium-sized
Recognized By	AKC, CKC, NZKC, KC, A
Life Span	12-14 years
Ideal Weight	Male: 50 Female: 40 pounds
Ideal Height	Male: 20 Female: 19 inches
Fur Type	Medium length, wavy or flat
Common Colors	Liver and White, Len

English Springer Spaniel

	Red and White, Black and V
Markings	Spotted, Roan, Ticked
Availability	Widely available
Achievements	Police dog
Suitable for Apartments	Yes
Used in World War	Helped front line soldier in
Most Similar To	English Cocker Spaniel

The English Springer Spaniels are keen, smart, and very active dogs. These dogs thrive on plenty of exercises. They are working dogs as well as a lovely companion in the house.

English Springer Spaniels are medium-size dogs with the typical gentle spaniel expression and drop ears. These breeds are gentle, affectionate and alert dogs which makes excellent watchdogs.

English Springer Spaniel

Characteristics of the English Springer Spaniel

English Spinger Spaniel

Maintenance: 🐾 🐾 🐾
Activity Level: 🐾 🐾 🐾 🐾
Kid Friendly: 🐾 🐾 🐾 🐾
Ease of Training: 🐾 🐾 🐾 🐾
Health Risks: 🐾 🐾 🐾

Affection Level	High
Friendliness	High
Kid-Friendly	High
Pet-Friendly	High
Exercise Needs	High
Playfulness	High
Energy Level	High

Trainability	High
Intelligence	High
Tendency to Bark	Medium
Amount of Shedding	Medium

History of the English Springer Spaniel

Dogs similar to the English Springer Spaniel (ESS) are seen in artwork as far back as the 16th century, but it wasn't until the early 19th century that their specific history can be identified.

Cocker Spaniels and Welsh and English Springer Spaniels are all closely related, and in the early days of their history in Britain, they would be born from the same litter and then separated by size and color.

Originally the Cockers were used for hunting woodcock. The larger Springers would be used to jump up, or Spring, to flush the gamebirds up into the air for the hunters to then catch them with nets and, then later, the gun.

English Springer Spaniel

The first definitive strain of pure English Springer Spaniels can be traced back to 1812. A wealthy family called the Bougheys, in Shropshire, bred from a Spaniel called Mop I, and they continued to be passionate about the breed well into the 1900s.

The English Springer Spaniel gained recognition from the Kennel Club in the UK in 1902, and in 1913 the first ESS were imported to North America.

In 1927 the English Springer Field Trial Association (ESSFTA) was established as the parent club for the breed and, from here, their popularity grew quickly.

There are two types of English Springer Spaniel, although they aren't recognized as separate breeds. The Bench or Show ESS focuses on conformation, and they tend to be slightly larger with a heavier coat and a calmer personality. The working, field-type ESS is smaller, faster and more athletic, and tends to be busier than their larger relatives.

In 2018, the English Springer Spaniel was ranked as the 27th most popular breed by the American Kennel Club. Their fun-loving and affectionate personalities have won the hearts of many dog lovers, including Oprah Winfrey, George W Bush and Grace Kelly.

Because of their intelligence, sensitive nose and desire to work, they're also often used as scent work dogs for the police and for search and rescue missions.

General Appearance

It is reasonably lively, good-natured, innately docile, very active and cheerful. It is also intelligent, gentle, kind, helpful and obedient, dedicated owners and members of its family - an excellent companion dog. Timidity or aggression is totally unknown to it. It is friendly to people, including strangers, unexpected visits and children. The happiest is if it can be with the owner and his family members together. It does not have lack of courage, playfulness, skill and energy. It can be gentle and loving.

The other dogs and other animals it behaves friendly. It should be used to stay with pets since its youth, but with the birds, for example. Do not free fly your parrot. Its hunting instinct when it can see flying birds, it is extremely powerful.

Originally used as a hunting dog-leash to search and pointing small ground game (hare) from the shelter. It is currently used as a hunting dog mainly to snoop, pointing and over chasing game and bringing back a haul.

Body:

English springer spaniel is the highest of all British hunting Spaniel. Its body is compact, powerful, perfectly adapted to hunting on land and in water. Height at withers is approximately about 51 cm.

The skull should be moderately long, sufficiently broad, slightly arched above. From the muzzle to the skull rises and forms the front steeping (stop) and brow ridges that divide between the eyes front longitudinal furrow. It is backwards to the occiput gradually loses.

The occiput should not be too pronounced. Under the eyes it must be full filled it cannot be lapsed.

The muzzle is broad and deep, the length corresponding to the length of the skull. Deep (reaching low) upper lip gives it an angular shape. The nostrils are well open, lips quite distinctive, somewhat looser. Jaws must be powerful bite required a perfect, complete, correct. Cheeks should be flat.

Eyes are medium sized, almond shaped, dark hazel in colour, neither protruding nor sunken, well set in the orbit. The conjunctiva should not be seen eyelids it should fit closely to the eyeballs. The sight must

English Springer Spaniel

be nice.

The earlobes are suspended, appropriate length and width, set at eye level. Immediately adjacent to the head, covered with hair forming a nice "hinge".
The neck is strong and muscular, of good length, without dewlap on the throat, the neck slightly arched. Towards the head tapers.

The body must be strong, neither too short nor excessively long. The chest is deep and spacious, with a properly sprung ribs. Loins should be muscular, strong, slightly arched and tightly connected with the back and croup.

The tail is short. Always be low and should never be carried above the top line of the body. The bottom is clearly marked "flag" and still vividly moving from side to side.

The forelegs are straight, strong, strong bones. Shoulders should be oblique, so their peaks upwards and backwards. Elbows close to your chest, must be neither turned in nor out. Wrists are strong and flexible.

The hindquarters should be perpendicular to the ground, legs wide, muscular, powerful, knees and hocks moderately angulated. Coarse hocks are highly not acceptable. Feet must be "closed" (compact, with tightly knit toes), rounded, with strong and tall padded.

Hair is fitting, dense and resistant to the changes of weather, never wired. Longer on the ear lobe, where it forms a "curtain" on the back of the forelegs, which make up the "flags" on the backs of the thighs, where it forms a "pants" and on the bottom side of the body, where they form a "fringing". Colour is brown-and-white or black-and-white, or both i.e. brindle (tan points).

Temperament and Personality

Whether the English Springer is a hunting dog, a field trial competitor or a show dog, he is always a family dog. The English Springer is a loving companion who is happiest when he is with his people. He barks to warn them that someone is approaching the house, but it's more likely in anticipation of making a new friend than in warning. As befits a Sporting dog, he's curious, outgoing and active, but "hyper" is not a word that should be used to describe him. If he gets plenty of daily exercise and face time with his family, the English Springer is adaptable to any type of home, from a city apartment to a sprawling ranch.

English Springer Spaniel

As a hunting dog, the English Springer has plenty of stamina and great scenting ability and retrieving skills. Field trial English Springers are athletes designed for speed and style. English Springers from show lines can hunt, but they are slower and more methodical than the field trial English Springers. All of those skills can be channeled in a English Springer who is a companion to make him a great competitor in dog sports such as agility, flyball, dock diving, rally, tracking and obedience.

Whether he comes from hunting lines or show lines, an English

Springer is highly intelligent and trainable. He has a natural desire to chase down prey and flush birds and those instincts must be molded by the hunter so the dog learns to focus on the appropriate types of birds or other game, but he learns quickly and remembers what he learns.

The perfect English Springer doesn't come ready-made from the breeder. Any dog, no matter how nice, can develop obnoxious levels of barking, digging, counter surfing and other undesirable behaviors if he is bored, untrained or unsupervised. And any dog can be a trial to live with during adolescence. In the case of the English Springer, the "teen" years can start at six months and continue until the dog is about 18 months old.

Start training your puppy the day you bring him home. Even at eight weeks old, he is capable of soaking up everything you can teach him. Don't wait until he is 6 months old to begin training or you will have a more headstrong dog to deal with. If possible, get him into puppy kindergarten class by the time he is 10 to 12 weeks old, and socialize, socialize, socialize. However, be aware that many puppy training classes require certain vaccines (like kennel cough) to be up to date, and many veterinarians recommend limited exposure to other dogs and public places until puppy vaccines (including rabies, distemper and parvovirus) have been completed. In lieu of formal training, you can begin training your puppy at home and socializing him among family and friends until puppy vaccines are completed.

Talk to the breeder, describe exactly what you're looking for in a dog, and ask for assistance in selecting a puppy. Breeders see the puppies daily and can make uncannily accurate recommendations once they know something about your lifestyle and personality.

The perfect English Springer doesn't spring fully formed from the whelping box. He's a product of his background and breeding. Whatever you want from an English Springer, look for one whose parents have nice personalities and who has been well socialized from early puppyhood.

Your English Springer Spaniel's Health

We know that because you care so much about your dog, you want to take good care of her. That is why we have summarized the health concerns we will be discussing with you over the life of your Springer Spaniel. By knowing about health concerns specific to English Springer Spaniels, we can tailor a preventive health plan to watch for and hopefully prevent some predictable risks.

Many diseases and health conditions are genetic, meaning they are related to your pet's breed. There is a general consensus among canine genetic researchers and veterinary practitioners that the conditions we've described herein have a significant rate of incidence and/or impact in this breed. That does not mean your dog will have these problems; it just means that she is more at risk than other dogs. We will describe the most common issues seen in English Springer Spaniels to give you an idea of what may come up in her future. Of course, we can't cover every possibility here, so always check with us if you notice any unusual signs or symptoms.

This guide contains general health information important to all canines as well as the most important genetic predispositions for English Springer Spaniels. This information helps you and us together plan for your pet's unique medical needs.

English Springer Spaniel

General Health Information for your English Springer Spaniel

Dental Disease

Dental disease is the most common chronic problem in pets, affecting 80% of all dogs by age two. Unfortunately, your English Springer Spaniel is more likely than other dogs to have problems with her teeth. Dental disease starts with tartar build-up on the teeth and progresses to infection of the gums and roots of the teeth. If we don't prevent or treat dental disease, your buddy may lose her teeth and be in danger of damage to her kidneys, liver, heart, and joints. In fact, your Spaniel's life span may even be cut short by one to three years! We'll clean your dog's teeth regularly and let you know what you can do at home to keep those pearly whites clean.

Infections

English Springer Spaniels are susceptible to bacterial and viral infections—the same ones that all dogs can get—such as parvo, rabies, and distemper. Many of these infections are preventable through vaccination, which we will recommend based on her age, the diseases we see in our area, and other factors.

Obesity

Obesity can be a significant health problem in English Springer Spaniels. It is a serious disease that may cause or worsen joint problems, metabolic and digestive disorders, back pain, and heart disease. Though it's tempting to give your pal food when she looks at you with those soulful eyes, you can "love her to death" with leftover people food and doggie treats. Instead, give her a hug, brush her fur or teeth, play a game with her, or perhaps take her for a walk. She'll feel better, and so will you!

Parasites

All kinds of worms and bugs can invade your Springer's body, inside and out. Everything from fleas and ticks to ear mites can infest her skin and ears. Hookworms, roundworms, heartworms, and whipworms can get into her system in a number of ways: drinking unclean water, walking on contaminated soil, or being bitten by an infected mosquito. Some of these parasites can be transmitted to you or a family member and are a serious concern for everyone. For your canine friend, these parasites can cause pain, discomfort, and even death, so it's important that we test for them on a regular basis. We'll also recommend preventive medication as necessary to keep her healthy.

Spay or Neuter

One of the best things you can do for your Springer Spaniel is to have her spayed (neutered for males). In females, this means we surgically remove the ovaries and usually the uterus, and in males, it means we surgically remove the testicles. Spaying or neutering decreases the likelihood of certain types of cancers and eliminates the possibility of your pet becoming pregnant or fathering unwanted puppies. Performing this surgery also gives us a chance, while your pet is under anesthesia, to identify and address some of the diseases your dog is likely to develop. For example, if your pet needs hip X-rays or a puppy tooth extracted, this would be a good time—it's more convenient for you and easier on your friend too. Routine blood testing prior to surgery also helps us to identify and take precautions against common problems that increase anesthetic or surgical risk. Don't worry; your Seven Hills Veterinary Hospital, Inc team is happy to discuss the specific problems we will be looking for when the time arrives.

Genetic Predispositions for English Springer Spaniels

Eye Problems

Not many things have as dramatic an impact on your dog's quality of life as the proper functioning of his eyes. Unfortunately, English Springer Spaniels can inherit or develop a number of different eye conditions, some of which may cause blindness if not treated right away, and most of which can be extremely painful! We will evaluate his eyes at every examination to look for any signs for concern.

- Glaucoma, an eye condition that affects English Springer Spaniels and people too, is an extremely painful disease that rapidly leads to blindness if left untreated. Symptoms include squinting, watery eyes, bluing of the cornea (the clear front part of the eye), and redness in the whites of the eyes. Pain is rarely noticed by pet owners though it is frequently there and can be severe. People who have certain types of glaucoma often report it feels like being stabbed in the eye with an ice pick! Yikes! In advanced cases, the eye may look enlarged or swollen like it's bulging. We'll perform an annual glaucoma screening to diagnose and start treatment as early as possible. Glaucoma is a medical emergency. If you see symptoms, don't wait to call us, go to an emergency clinic!

- Cataracts are a common cause of blindness in older Springer Spaniels. We'll watch for the lenses of his eyes to become more opaque—meaning they look cloudy instead of clear—when we examine him. Many dogs adjust well to losing their vision and get along just fine. Surgery to remove cataracts and restore sight may also be an option.

English Springer Spaniel

- Progressive retinal atrophy (PRA) is an inherited disease in which the eyes are genetically programmed to go blind. Unfortunately, English Springer Spaniels are a bit more likely than other dogs to have this condition. PRA is not painful, but also not curable. In dogs with this gene, early symptoms such as night blindness or dilated pupils generally begin around three to five years of age. A genetic test is available for this condition.

Heart Disease

English Springer Spaniel

Some breeds, like your Springer Spaniel, can be born with a variety of heart defects. Most affect the structure of the heart's dividing wall or the vessels of the heart. Defects can also cause problems with heart valve function or the electrical signals that control the heartbeat. Because of the significant risk of heart disease in this breed, we'll pay special attention to his heart during each examination. Special testing will be recommended if we hear a heart murmur or if you notice any unusual symptoms such as tiring easily, coughing, a swollen belly, or fainting.

- Springer Spaniels are susceptible to a condition called patent ductus arteriosis, or PDA, in which a small vessel that carries blood between two parts of the heart does not close as it should shortly after birth. This results in too much blood being carried to the lungs, causing fluid build-up and strain on the heart. Outward signs may be mild or severe, including coughing, fatigue during exercise, weight loss, shortness of breath, and weakness in the hind limbs. We listen for a specific type of heart murmur to diagnose this problem during your pet's examinations. If your pal has this condition, we may recommend surgery to close the problematic vessel.

Diabetes

Diabetes mellitus is a fairly common disease in dogs. Any breed can be affected, but Springers have an above average incidence. Dogs with diabetes are unable to regulate the metabolism of sugars in their bodies and require daily insulin injections. Diabetes is a serious condition and one that is important to diagnose and treat as early as possible. Symptoms include increased eating, drinking, and urination, along with weight loss. If he shows signs, we will conduct lab tests to determine if he has this condition and discuss treatment options with you. Treatment requires a serious commitment of time and resources. Well-regulated diabetic dogs today have the same life expectancy as other canines.

Ear Infections

Allergies, swimming, overgrowth of hair in the ear canals, and accumulation of earwax can all predispose your dog to ear infections, which are painful and annoying. Springer Spaniels are very often afflicted by allergies, which can cause itching and inflammation in the ears and elsewhere. The earlier we diagnose and treat these ailments, the less discomfort and pain your pet will suffer. Be sure to call us if you notice him scratching or shaking his head, a foul odor from the ears, or if his ears seem painful to the touch. By monitoring for ear infections and treating them early, we also reduce the likelihood of eardrum damage that can lead to deafness. Most ear infections tend to recur until we work together to control the underlying cause.

Bleeding Disorders

There are several types of inherited bleeding disorders that occur in dogs. They range in severity from very mild to very severe. Many times a pet seems normal until a serious injury occurs or surgery is performed, and then severe bleeding can result. English Springer Spaniels are particularly prone to some relatively rare diseases of the blood.

- Hemolytic anemia and thrombocytopenia occur when the immune system goes haywire and starts attacking the pet's own red blood cells or platelets. If the immune system destroys red blood cells, your dog quickly becomes anemic, weak, and lethargic. His gums will look whitish or yellow instead of a normal bright pink color. If the immune system destroys platelets, his blood won't clot properly and he'll have bruises or abnormal bleeding. We'll perform diagnostic testing for blood clotting to check for these problems before we perform any surgeries. To slow or stop the immune system's destruction of cells, we'll prescribe steroids and other immune-suppressive drugs. Sometimes an emergency transfusion of red blood cells or platelets is needed.

- Von Willebrand's disease is a blood clotting disorder frequently found in English Springer Spaniels. We'll conduct diagnostic testing for blood clotting times or a specific DNA blood test for Von Willebrand's disease and other similar disorders to check for this problem before we perform surgery.

PFK Deficiency

Phosphofructokinase (PFK) Deficiency, also known as Tauri disease or glycogen storage disease, is a genetic defect that affects the body's metabolism of glucose. Symptoms appear anywhere from 2-3 months to several years of age, and include exercise intolerance, anemia, fever, and muscle disease. Fortunately, a DNA test is available to help diagnose this life-limiting disease. Because your English Springer Spaniel is at risk for PFK Deficiency, we will keep a watchful eye on him during his early years.

Cancer

Cancer is a leading cause of death among dogs in their golden years. Your English Springer Spaniel is a bit more prone to certain kinds of cancer starting at a younger age. Many cancers are curable by surgical removal, and some types are treatable with chemotherapy. Early detection is critical! We'll do periodic blood tests and look for lumps and bumps at each exam.

Neurologic Problems

Several neurologic diseases can afflict English Springer Spaniels. Symptoms of neurological problems can include seizures, imbalance, tremors, weakness, or excessive sleeping. If you notice any of these symptoms, please seek immediate veterinary care.

Epilepsy

There are three types of seizures in dogs: reactive, secondary, and primary. Reactive seizures are caused by the brain's reaction to a metabolic problem like low blood sugar, organ failure, or a toxin. Secondary seizures are the result of a brain tumor, stroke, or trauma. If no other cause can be found, the disease is called primary or idiopathic epilepsy. This problem is often an inherited condition, and English Springer Spaniels are commonly afflicted. If your friend is prone to seizures, episodes will usually begin between six months and three years of age. An initial diagnostic workup may help find the cause. Lifelong medication is usually necessary to help keep seizures under control with periodic blood testing required to monitor side effects and efficacy. If your dog has a seizure,carefully prevent him from injuring himself, but don't try to control his mouth or tongue. It won't help him, and he may bite you accidentally! Note the length of the seizure, and call us or an emergency hospital.

Rage Syndrome

Rage syndrome, also called Springer Rage, is a dangerous form of dominance aggression that is thought to be a form of epilepsy. English Springer Spaniels with this condition have episodes of extreme aggression, often attacking their owners. Affected dogs may respond positively to anti-seizure medications, but they should never be used for breeding!

Hip and Elbow Dysplasia

Both hips and elbows are at risk for dysplasia, an inherited disease that causes the joints to develop improperly and results in arthritis. Stiffness in your Springer Spaniel's elbows or hips may become a problem for him, especially as he matures. You may notice that he begins to show lameness in his legs or has difficulty getting up from lying down. We can treat the arthritis—the sooner the better—to minimize discomfort and pain. We'll take X-rays of your dog's bones to identify issues as early as possible. Surgery is also sometimes a good option in severe and life-limiting cases. And keep in mind that overweight dogs may develop arthritis years earlier than those of normal weight, causing undue pain and suffering!

Bone Pain

Growing Springer Spaniels can suffer from a painful inflammation of the long bones in the legs called eosinophilic panosteitis, or pano or eo-pan for short. It usually starts around six to ten months of age and shifts from leg to leg. We'll look for this condition upon examination; if your pal exhibits pain when the area is squeezed or palpated, we'll take X-rays to diagnose the problem. Panosteitis usually causes no permanent damage, but requires pain medication. If your dog has this condition and develops an abnormal gait to compensate for the sore leg(s), rehabilitation exercises may be required.

Skin Disease

Seborrhea is a common skin disease that can cause dry, flaky skin, called seborrhea sicca, or greasy, oily skin, called seborrhea oleosa. Both forms can make your pet itchy and uncomfortable, and skin infections are more likely to occur. Seborrhea is among the most annoying of diseases to Springer Spaniel owners because it often makesaffected pets smelly and unattractive. Hypothyroidism (low thyroid hormone levels) can lead to seborrhea, as can allergies, Cushing's disease, and other problems.

Autoimmune Skin Disease

Pemphigus foliaceus is a superficial skin disease that is more common in English Springer Spaniels. It often starts around four years of age and causes crusts and hair loss, usually on top of the nose and inside the ear flaps. Some dogs get it on their footpads and toenails as well. Bacteria easily invade the damaged areas, so secondary skin infections are common. Skin crusts typically wax and wane; there is no cure, but there are a variety of effective treatments. Sunlight makes it worse, so applying zinc-free sunscreen to sensitive parts before heading outdoors can help.

Taking Care of Your English Springer Spaniel at Home

Much of what you can do to keep your dog happy and healthy is common sense, just like it is for people. Watch her diet, make sure she gets plenty of exercise, regularly brush her teeth and coat, and call us or a pet emergency hospital when something seems unusual (see "What to Watch For" below). Be sure to adhere to the schedule of examinations and vaccinations that we recommend for her. This is when we'll give her the necessary "check-ups" and test for diseases and conditions that are common in Springer Spaniels. Another very important step in caring for your pet is signing up for pet health insurance. There will certainly be medical tests and procedures she will need throughout her life and pet health insurance will help you cover those costs.

Routine Care, Diet, and Exercise

Build her routine care into your schedule to help your Springer live longer, stay healthier, and be happier during her lifetime. We cannot overemphasize the importance of a proper diet and exercise routine.

- Supervise your pet as you would a toddler. Keep doors closed, pick up after yourself, and block off rooms as necessary. This will keep her out of trouble and away from objects she shouldn't put in her mouth.

English Springer Spaniel

- Daily brushing and regular trimming is recommended to prevent mats and keep her long coat beautiful.

- English Springer Spaniels generally have good teeth, and you can keep them perfect by brushing them at least twice a week!

- Clean her ears weekly, even as a puppy. Make sure to keep her floppy ears dry. Don't worry—we'll show you how!

- She is a highly active dog that excels at dog sports like flyball, agility, dock diving, and field trials, so keep her exercised!

- She is a high-energy hunting dog, so a fenced yard and leashed walks are a must.

- She loves the water!And swimming is a great form of exercise for your English Springer Spaniel.

- Keep your dog's diet consistent and don't give her people food.

- Feed a high-quality diet appropriate for her age.

- Exercise your dog regularly, but don't overdo it at first.

What to Watch For

English Springer Spaniel

Any abnormal symptom could be a sign of serious disease or it could just be a minor or temporary problem. The important thing is to be able to tell when to seek veterinary help and how urgently. Many diseases cause dogs to have a characteristic combination of symptoms, which together can be a clear signal that your English Springer Spaniel needs help.

Office Calls

Give a call for an appointment if you notice any of these types of signs:

- Change in appetite or water consumption
- Tartar build-up, bad breath, red gums, or broken teeth

- Itchy skin (scratching, chewing, or licking); hair loss
- Lethargy, mental dullness, or excessive sleeping
- Fearfulness, aggression, or other behavioral changes
- Increased hunger and thirst, weight loss
- Sudden aggressive episodes with no apparent cause

Emergencies

Seek medical care immediately if you notice any of these types of signs:

- Scratching or shaking the head, tender ears, or ear discharge
- Inability or straining to urinate; discolored urine
- Cloudiness, redness, itching, or any other abnormality involving the eyes
- Fatigue during exercise, coughing, or shortness of breath
- Gums that are a color other than bright pink
- Tiring easily, coughing, a swollen belly or fainting/collapse

- General reluctance to run or play

- Any abnormal shaking, trembling, or excessive involuntary tremors

English Springer Spaniel Care

If you lead a quiet and sedentary lifestyle, then the English Springer Spaniel wouldn't be the best choice of dog for you.

If you're looking for a dog that loves to be in the company of humans and dogs alike, is smart and has bundles of energy to join you on long hikes and adventures, then you could be a perfect match.

A quick leash walk around the block before you head to work isn't enough for this dog, and it could lead to behavioral problems as a result of boredom. They also thrive in company and are best suited to a household where there will be someone around most of the day. They can be prone to separation anxiety.

If you enjoy hiking, running or cycling, then your ESS will be thrilled to accompany you. They're enthusiastic canicross competitors and often excel in agility, flyball, scent work trials and other competitive dog sports.

They love to be busy, have a job to do, and are extremely eager to please. This means they respond very well to reward-based training methods. They're very smart and pick up commands quickly.

Clear direction and patience can be needed sometimes, as their enthusiasm can mean they try to take things a little fast and they can be prone to overexcitement. You may have to work on mastering things like jumping up, excitement barking, leash manners, especially around other dogs, and even toilet training, as they can be prone to

English Springer Spaniel

piddling if over-excited.

English Springer Spaniels are often a popular choice for families with children or other dogs. They're very affectionate and are often regarded as 'velcro dogs', that always want to be close to their human companions.

Their natural excitement can mean they could be a bit boisterous for very young children, and you may need to work on encouraging them to keep all four paws on the floor, and even use management techniques like baby gates when you can't be there to supervise.

Their hunting background means they may want to chase small furries and care would need to be taken if you have small pets in the same household. You'll likely have to work on getting a rock-solid recall too.

An English Springer Spaniel won't have extremely intensive grooming requirements. The Bench or Show types may require extra brushing as their coat tends to be heavier.

They're moderate shedders, and a good weekly brush will help to keep loose hairs at bay and the coat in healthy condition. They can get mats around their ears and on their feathering more easily, and you should always pay extra attention to these areas when brushing.

Because of their pendulous ears, you should check these regularly to make sure they aren't becoming dirty, and this is especially true if they enjoy swimming. Dirt and water can get trapped more easily in their low hanging ears, and this can lead to ear infections if they aren't kept clean and dry.

Trainability

English Springer Spaniel

English Springer spaniels are easy to train because If you stay patient, put in efforts and show enough love then you will be able to train your dog. Some of the training tips are as follows:

Do not punish your English Springer Spaniel

When you are training your English Springer Spaniel dog never try to beat or punish the dog. This can make them scared and can hate you in your training so be aware while training.

Use a reward-based system of training

Reward based training is always a savior while training any dogs. Giving reward to your pet while training can help them to feel motivated and happy. They will willingly perform your commands just for the treats.

Use short, calm commands

When your English Springer Spaniel dog is not doing what they are supposed to do, express your unhappiness with sharp and short commands. This will make them do the works making it interesting rather than punishing them.

How much does an English Springer Spaniel cost?

Five adorable Springer Spaniel puppies sleeping in the field

The average price of an English Springer Spaniel is between **$700 and $1,000.**

Keep in mind that the cost will vary depending on the pup's gender and availability, the kennel's location, the breeder's popularity, and many more.

English Springer Spaniel

With that said, some can be really expensive, especially if they come from a line of champions.

Fun fact: English Springer Spaniels have an average litter size of 6 puppies.

It would be best if you also considered the expenses that come with owning this purebred. Besides grooming, feeding, and accessories, vaccinations and emergency visits to the vet can be costly.

If you're determined to own a Springer Spaniel of your own, let us help you find one that's for sale or adoption.

Pros

- Smart and eager to please
- Affectionate with people and other dogs
- Can be prone to separation anxiety

Cons

- Needs a lot of exercise and stimulation
- Can be over-excitable

- Can have a high prey drive

English Springer Spaniel breeders

It may seem easy to go online and browse kennels and breeders that have postings about their "English Springer Spaniels for sale."

But before you sign a contract and make a purchase, it's crucial that you do your research. Find out what their previous clients say about their experiences, and if possible, request to visit where the dogs are kept.

This will give you the opportunity to ask important questions and observe if the dogs are healthy and well cared for. You'll also see how the parents and puppies react when they see their owners and strangers.

Doing so will give you better chances in taking home a healthy and well-tempered doggo.

The first place we'll recommend for you to look at is the AKC Marketplace. English Springer Spaniel Field Trials also has a page with breeders and kennels.

If you're in the U.K., The English Springer Spaniel Club has a list of breed clubs that you can reach out to for a list of their members and breeders around their area.

English Springer Spaniel for adoption

People often have the idea that shelters and rescue organizations only care for mutts or crossbreeds, but purebreds can be found there, too.

Some people usually think English Springer Spaniels are cute as puppies, but once they realize that they can't handle their temperament or grooming requirements, they just leave them there to be rehomed.

So if you prefer adopting an older dog and you're willing to give a pooch another chance for a family and to be loved, check out these fur angels on these websites:

- English Springer Rescue America, Inc. (Woodstock, GA)
- Mid Atlantic English Springer Spaniel Rescue (Goochland, VA)
- New England English Springer Spaniel Rescue (Ashland, MA)

- Golden Gate Springer Rescue (Oakland, CA)
- English Springer Spaniel Club of Long Island – Rescue (Bayport, NY)

We recommend letting your local shelter know you are looking for an English Springer Spaniel if they currently don't have any springers you can adopt.

The verdict: Should you get an English Springer Spaniel?

An English Springer Spaniel smiling sweetly

English Springer Spaniel

English Springer Spaniels is a *challenging breed for first-time dog owners.*

They're clingy and don't like spending time alone, and they require a lot of attention in terms of grooming, training, and daily exercise.

The thing is, all that hard work will also result in a rewarding companion.

They're family- and pet-friendly, **intelligent fidos that are obedient** and can excel in canine sports and as service dogs.

They're sociable, too. So when you have guests, or you live in a busy part of the city or town, you don't have to worry about owning this springer.

Springer Spaniels also love being busy, and if you have a pool or live near the ocean or lake, this pooch loves to swim.

Despite its high energy, the English Springer Spaniel is an excellent breed of dog for new and experienced owners that can dedicate their time and attention to this fido.

Do you have a springer in your family? Tell us about your experience in the comments below.

English Springer Spaniel

Further reading: Similar breeds to the English Springer Spaniel

- American Cocker Spaniel
- Welsh Springer Spaniel
- Field Spaniel
- Sussex Spaniel
- Clumber Spaniel
- Cavalier King Charles Spaniel

How to Identify an English Springer Spaniel

English Springer Spaniels are hunting dogs, and members of the Sporting Group. Although they share some characteristics with other dog breeds, they have some characteristics that are unique to them as well.

Method 1: Looking at the Body Structure

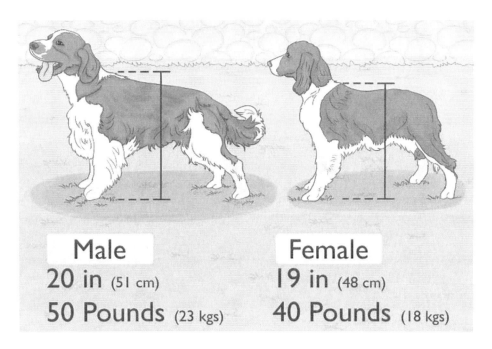

Male
20 in (51 cm)
50 Pounds (23 kgs)

Female
19 in (48 cm)
40 Pounds (18 kgs)

See what the dog's size is. Male English Springer Spaniels are usually around 20 inches (51 cm) tall, and they usually weigh around 50 pounds (23 kg), while female English Springer Spaniels are slightly smaller, usually being around 19 inches (48 cm) tall, and they weigh approximately 40 pounds (18 kg).

Note the dog's head overall. English Springer Spaniels should have a head that appears to be around the same length as its neck, and it has a relatively broad-shaped skull of medium length, that appears flat on the top, and is rounded slightly at its sides and back.

English Springer Spaniel

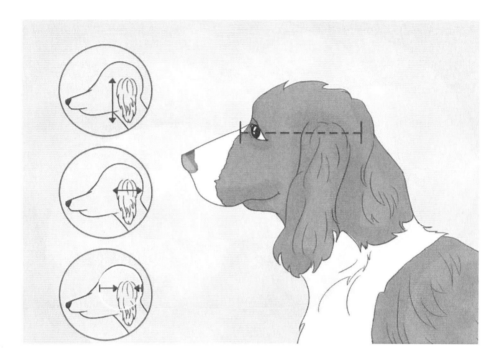

Check the dog's ears. English Springer Spaniels should have ears that are set at about eye-level, not too far back on their skull, long, and relatively wide. They should also not stand out or upwards, and they should be hanging close to the dog's cheeks. In addition, you should notice thin ear leather that appears long enough to reach the tip of the dog's nose.

Examine the dog's eyes. English Springer Spaniels should have eyes that are set well-apart from each other, and deep in their sockets.

They should also be oval-shaped and medium-sized.

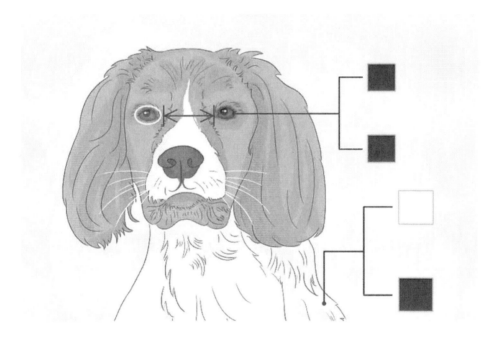

- The eye color will depend on the dog's coat color (likely a black or dark brown color in black and white dogs, or a darker shade of hazel in liver and white-colored dogs).

Look at the dog's nose. English Springer Spaniels have well-opened, broad nostrils on their nose, and it should be either black or liver in color, depending on the dog's coat color.

See what the dog's tail looks like. English Springer Spaniels carry their tails either horizontally or elevated slightly, and in a merry, lively manner.

- The tail may also be docked.

View the dog's overall appearance. Overall, English Springer Spaniels should appear balanced and well-proportioned, with a long, smooth, effortless gait.

Method 2: Noticing the Coat

Know the possible color combinations that an English Springer Spaniel may be. There are a few different possible color combinations you may notice on an English Springer Spaniel, and they include:

- Black and white
- Liver and white
- Mostly white with liver or black markings

English Springer Spaniel

- Liver roan

- Blue

- Tricolor (black or liver and white, with tan-colored markings)

Look for feathering. English Springer Spaniels typically have areas of feathering of moderate length and moderate heaviness on their brisket, chest, legs and ears.

Examine the coat's overall appearance. Overall, English Springer Spaniels should have a medium-sized outer-coat that is either flat or wavy, and a dense, soft and short undercoat. Their coat as a whole should have a glossy and clean appearance.

Method 3: Checking Temperament

Notice if the dog is affectionate. English Springer Spaniels are known to be very affectionate dogs.

Look for cheerfulness. English Springer Spaniels are also known to be cheerful, bubbly dogs who can put a smile on people's faces

English Springer Spaniel

Check if the dog is people-oriented. English Springer Spaniels are very people-oriented, meaning that they love being around people, and don't like being left alone.

See if the dog is very intelligent. English Springer Spaniels are known to be very intelligent dogs, which also makes them relatively easy to train.

Notice attentiveness. Another thing that makes English Springer Spaniels relatively easy to train is the fact that they are attentive.

Figure out if the dog is active. English Springer Spaniels are very active dogs, who aren't too content lounging, and instead would rather be running around outside.

- Because they are active, they require a lot of exercise, even through things like daily walks, games of fetch, or time to run in a fenced-in yard.

Note any alertness. English Springer Spaniels are known to be alert dogs, ready to jump into action when it is necessary.

Tips

- If you're wondering whether or not your dog is an English Springer Spaniel, consider a dog DNA test. This will help confirm your dog's breed.

Manufactured by Amazon.ca
Acheson, AB